PEACE, LOVE, HAPPINESS, AND JOY FOR THE UNIVERSE

GLENN SIMPSON

authorHOUSE®

AuthorHouse™
1663 Liberty Drive
Bloomington, IN 47403
www.authorhouse.com
Phone: 1 (800) 839-8640

Published by AuthorHouse 02/28/2019

ISBN: 978-1-5462-7491-9 (sc)
ISBN: 978-1-5462-7490-2 (hc)
ISBN: 978-1-5462-7492-6 (e)

Library of Congress Control Number: 2019900764

Print information available on the last page.

This book is printed on acid-free paper.

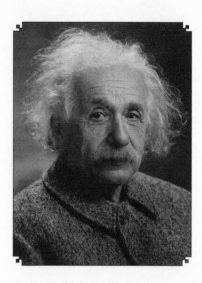

I want to know God's thoughts—the rest are details.

—Albert Einstein

If I have seen further than other [people] it is
because I have stood on the shoulders of giants.

—Sir Isaac Newton

To my family, including my late parents, James and Helen; my brothers, Donald and Duncan; my oldest niece, Meredith, and her husband, Josh; my youngest niece, Rebecca; my grandniece, Fiona; my sister-in-law, Jenny; and my aunts, uncles, and cousins, especially Celeste Seymour Grulick and her daughters, Victoria and Valerie, and Steve and Madelyn. And a special thanks to my family friends Helga and Bobbi.

To all the people who love God, themselves, and their neighbors. And to everyone else too.

To all living creatures in this universe and any other universes that may exist.

CONTENTS

ACKNOWLEDGMENTS

My Unitarian Universalist Minister Dr. Steven Meredith Garmon, without whose advice this book would not have been possible. Truly a Unitarian Universalist gentleman and a hero among all people.

Cindy Peterson-Dana for her mentoring, wisdom, and patience—and because she always gave me hope and never gave up on me.

Thom Federn for his unconditional positive regard and extreme intellect, knowledge, and wisdom.

My special friends Norma, Justin, Carol, Paula, and Lisa.

My publishing consultant, Chase Bay, who whipped me into shape—although sometimes a bit too much, perhaps. I appreciate it anyway.

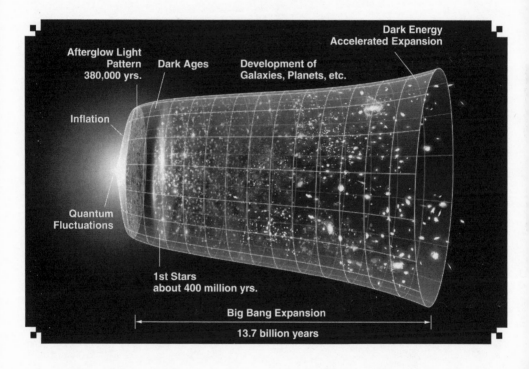

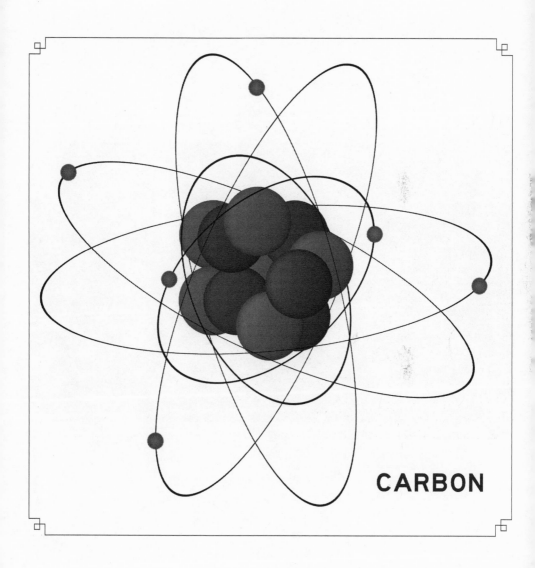

CARBON

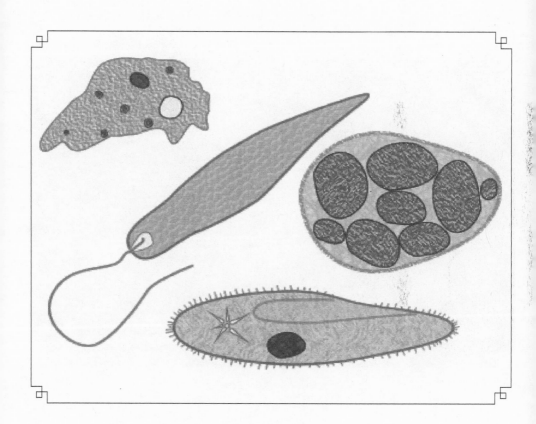

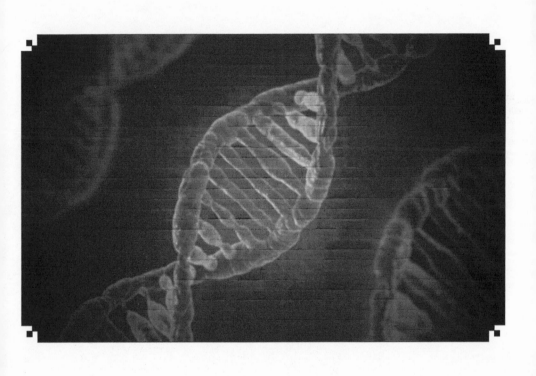

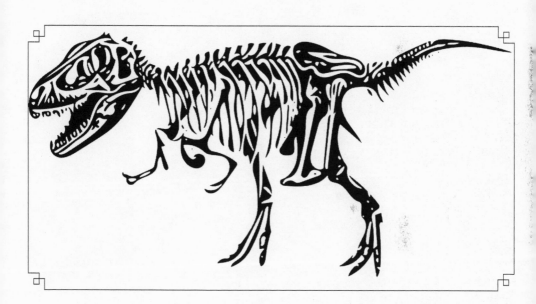

INTRODUCTION

You may be curious about the title.

Let's take the first part of the main title, "Peace, Love, Happiness, and Joy," first.

Why did I use these specific words in this particular order?

First off, peace is required before love and happiness can grow fully. *Peace* here refers to both internal and external peace. (Of course, war interferes with peace. War is hell.)

Love treats each individual with his or her best interests at heart. Peace and love together are the best chance for happiness in this world of ours. We need to love ourselves first to share love with others. Happiness can be a choice. Joy is increased happiness!

I take little credit for this analysis or anything in this book. For example, it was written thousands of years ago in the Old Testament of the Bible to obey the law. That helps us achieve peace. And therein also was written in many places to love God and our neighbor as ourselves, especially in the New Testament. So peace and love are each the outcome of following the Old and New Testaments separately, and happiness is the outcome of this peace and love taken together.

But what if you, the reader, don't believe in God or you are agnostic? That's not a problem. Many say that God is love. So, even if you don't believe in God (or even if you do), you can still love love itself.

I've attempted to write this book with special attention to each person as an individual and all people in the world entirely within the universe.

An unknown Russian philosopher wrote, "The power of ideas is greater than the use of force." It's my hope that all the ideas in this book will come down to personal choice. I hope one day you will choose at the election polls in the United States and everywhere else. With this knowledge, we will move toward individual peace, love, happiness, and joy and, in so doing, move toward these things together.

THIS IS A HANDBOOK FOR LIVING

Let's look at the beginning of this book like a road map.

OUR STARTING POINT

Here in this country and elsewhere, there are weapons of mass destruction and threats of their use—nuclear, biological, and chemical weapons. Gun violence is rampant in the United States too. Didn't Rodney King say, "Why can't we just get along?" If Jesus Christ could say, "Forgive them, Lord, for they no not what they do," after all that was done to him, why can't we at the very least do the same and resolve what often may be our profoundly petty differences in comparison?

There is war right now. Look at Syria as one example. There is terrorism; starvation; a lack of water, shelter, and medicine; sex slavery; and crime. There's corruption in business and government. There are countless types of violence; torture, political imprisonment, and death. There is neglect, abuse, rape, incest, and discrimination based on sex, age, race, national origin, sexual preference, and more. And there are environmental issues, including pollution and global warming. Many countries are near or at default, and the United States and other countries have serious financial problems and areas of overpopulation within them. ISIS and al-Qaeda make war in the name of forcing their religion on others (exactly as we did with the American Indian and with the Crusades in the name of the doctrine of discovery – wherein the victors over those having a so-called "lesser God" obtain their land).

THE END POINT OR GOAL

Imagine a nearly utopian world. Everyone has freedom of choice, except to break the law. If you break the law, there are consequences, if only in the conscience. The goal is peace, love, happiness, and joy for everyone (and, of course, a *much* a higher standard of living for all of us).

No one can make it happen alone. But we can all think globally, act locally, and try to act like a team. We won't know whether we can do it unless we try. The rewards are beyond anyone's hitherto understanding.

Let's start with world peace. If there's a nuclear holocaust, the only love will be from God. There won't be any life for millennia—at least aboveground. What if God said, "This is my ball, and if I don't like the way you play with it, I will take it away from all of you. Maybe with an asteroid from outer space!"? Think about it. It is said in the Bible that God sets before us life and death – and to choose life. I think God also sets before us good and evil, and I suggest that we all choose good. But we all have freedom of choice. My late father used to say, "You can do anything in this life—if you can accept the consequences."

Some people say that the next world war will be waged over food because the world population is growing faster than the food supply.

WHAT ROUTE DO WE TAKE?

Choose peace first of all … and unite. Two heads are better than one, they say. Those who agree with this book may possibly make their best vote ever. They may choose to elect a presidential candidate for the United States who runs on a platform of seeking to form a united world government led by a world leader who demonstrates how we can solve every problem caused by humankind. We want these propositions in writing so that the candidate can't go back on his or her promises about them later.

Of course, this person wouldn't be God. But some people may perhaps in some cases believe that he or she is the resurrection of Jesus Christ or at least an entity that deserves some small amount of respect. Thank God we have religious freedom in this country (theoretically), freedom of the press (theoretically), and equal rights (on paper).

Perhaps this country can be whipped into shape by the next president. And then other countries will be attracted to our new form of government and join us. But why should they try right now? After all, we have more violence and imprisonment than any other country.

There is a European Union. The United States belongs to NATO. There is the United Nations. The United States of America was formed long ago. I believe this all gives credence to the idea that we are stronger together than separately.

A one-world government has been prophesied throughout the Bible. And I believe other religions and organizations have done so too (see https://www.tomorrowsworld.org/magazines/2018/july-august/the-coming-one-world-government). In the article it is said that we should look for signs of Jesus Christ. Of course, Jesus died on the cross a long time ago. I think it's best to look for the resurrection or second coming ... or something better. Perhaps we should turn to a Unitarian Universalist – a liberal religion that accepts people of all faiths, including atheists and agnostics. What do you think? It's all quite simple. The most complicated ideas in physics all follow the scientific method. There's no magic.

It seems to me it is of little matter what religion or nonreligious organizations we choose – if they are nonviolent. It's a strategy to save ourselves from nuclear holocaust that could occur at any moment. A supersonic jet with nuclear cluster bombs could fly over your house right now. And what are we going do about it? Please understand. I've done my research and gone into debt to self-publish. And my time matters—at least it does to me. And I may not make one penny in royalties. I may not live to see any of this happen. But I hope someday you will see world peace—for your sake. I certainly don't plan to leave anyone out, and I'm never going to stop as long as I live. So take it or leave it. Didn't Christopher Columbus and the Pilgrims take much bigger risks? And look what happened.

What's the methodology for joining this new united world government? Generally, the most prosperous countries would be asked to join first, while we join military forces (enabling a reduced military budget overall). Then all the democratic countries would join and be led by this world leader I've mentioned.

That next US president would sign into law an amendment to our constitution to read, "We the People of the United World Government" instead of "We the People of the United States of America." Perhaps people will write to, call, and vote for senators and congresspeople who will vote for this as well. I don't know. Maybe I'm just barking up the wrong tree. At least I know I'm trying. I won't be happy until everyone has peace, love, happiness, and joy.

Yes, my idea is to overthrow the government of the United States of America—without the use of force but with the power of our minds, bodies, hearts, and souls in the hope of a better life for all Americans and all people. This would be a win-win situation for everyone. Don't worry. Our love will not hurt us. Just be true to yourself and do not diminish yourself in your love. It works. I myself have suffered much anguish, and yet I am very peaceful, loving, happy, and joyful. And I try my best to stay that way and become even better and help others be the same.

The first goal of the world leader would be world peace. Think of the money we could save with economies of scale and smaller government, more cooperative business alliances, and less spending on military. If there were a world government with lasting peace, it would be less necessary to support traumatized war veterans and their families. We're still deciding on financial reparations for Holocaust survivors and families.

I believe in one government, tolerance for all religions, and nonviolence, not big government but smaller overall with less redundancy. The savings should help bring up the standard of living for everyone so that we can eventually help poorer countries with our surplus. Make America better than it ever was before.

It may be that not everyone *wants* peace, love, happiness, and joy. I believe that's what people *need* after their basic needs are met.

REASONING

My expert leadership professor at Duke University's Fuqua School of Business in Durham, North Carolina, taught our class that the strongest force in an organization is equity and that the worst emotion is regret. We can all be more peaceful, loving, happy, and joyful than we are now. We can choose not to hurt ourselves and others. We can always choose to do nothing if the only other alternatives are to do harm to ourselves or others. We can admit our mistakes, confess any wrongdoing, and try to make amends. In the Bible, it's called *repentance*.

My quantitative analysis professor at Duke introduced himself to the class as a former presidential advisor in the navy. He told us that his computer-based linear-programming model was accepted by the president back then to create the so-called fail-safe mechanism used to position our nuclear submarines around the world. The goal was to maximize destruction with the press of the infamous *button* available to the president. So I believe that button exists. It's a reality. Now I think that very same program in conjunction with other programs I learned about at Duke and in business could be used to help maximize happiness in the United States and in other countries throughout the world. For example, we could analyze instead where to distribute surplus food, shelter, clothes, medicine, and other needs, which should help lead us toward lasting peace, love, and happiness, and joy.

The professor used an acronym to explain to the class a three-pronged tactic for persuasion—EEL, which refers to external, explicit, and logical. Counter the worst critics first.

In addition to personal and family safety, world peace would also achieve economic saving and prevent incalculable human suffering. Here's some research on the economic aspects of war.

> A report in May 2011 on the Global Peace Index highlighted that if the world had been 25% more peaceful in the past year, the global

economy would have benefited by an additional $2 trillion, which would account for 2% of global GDP per annum required to mitigate global warming, cover all costs to achieve the Millennium Development Goals, cancel all public debt held by Greece, Ireland, and Portugal, and cover the rebuilding costs for the 2011 Thoko earthquake and tsunami.[1]

That's only 25 percent. That's not my goal at all. My goal is 100 percent peace and not just between countries and civil war. I'm talking about society—and nothing less. If everyone just called a truce, declared peace, laid down their weapons, and chose nonviolence, then war and other negatives would, of course, lessen. It starts with individuals, families, and parents and goes all the way up to countries and their leadership, including dictators and terrorist groups.

In psychology there is something called the "cycle of abuse." For instance, a perpetrator may think, *It's been done to me, so I'm going to do it to you.* Breaking that kind of vicious cycle

---

[1] http://en.wikipedia.org/wiki/World_peace#cite_note-22.

requires one to think, *It's been done to me, but I'm not going to do it to anyone else. I will learn from it. It is an opportunity to learn.*

Talk to your family, and don't forget to listen. Speak to representatives in the government and the United Nations to work out grievances. There's always a peaceful solution. Children will hopefully inherit this earth. Please listen to them if not to me.

BASIC NEEDS

If peacekeeping savings were spent on basic needs, there would be less inequity and less reason for war. Didn't Hitler rise to power based on a promise to feed his country's hungry people? After the Nuremberg trials, didn't we say, "Never again?" Genocide is going on right now. The United States entered World War II much too late.

The psychologist Abraham Maslow postulated a "hierarchy of needs." The first set of needs is food, shelter, clothing, medicine, and security. We need to satisfy those needs first before we attain what he described as "self-actualization," which I define as the most peaceful, loving, happy, and joyous growth. It's been said that if love doesn't grow, it dies.

Democracy, communism, and socialism all have their good points and weak points. Democracy gives everyone an equal vote. That's fantastic. But we know that here in America, there are also many forms of inequality and unequal opportunity. There's even imbalance in the opportunity to vote.

Communism allows people to work according to their abilities and to receive according to need. The theory is great, but in practice, it can be abused.

Socialism has people work according to their abilities and receive according to their contribution. I think communism and socialism can be combined. Everyone could work according to ability and receive based on both contribution and need.

We could take the very best of all systems, particularly those of the United Nations.

I don't know all the answers—no one does—but let's see how we can help make this system work like a happy marriage and family.

I am just a layperson and am only going by what I've read and heard. Let's take the question of Israel and Palestine in the Middle East. To start, we must first be like doctors who pledge to "first do no harm." People are living where they are. Let's go from there. "Thou shalt not steal" land or "kill." Be humane. I don't believe any land is *promised* just because it says so in a religious book. Where's the deed? Did their adversaries pay for the land? Is it owed in monetary terms? Is this religious book a contract voluntarily entered into by all parties? Anyone can write a book full of promises. And we can all be just at the very least.

Be in the here and now, and try to stop living in the past. The past is over. All we can do is learn from it. Learn from the past, live in the now, and dream of the future. Plan for peace, love, happiness, and joy. Have you ever heard of self-fulfilling prophecies that have both positive and negative consequences? If you prophesy that your world will become more positive, you will see more opportunities to make it so and choose more wisely to make it happen. The converse is also true.

That's as far as the land goes. War crimes must be judged and punished, especially for the sake of the living, either in the countries in which they were committed or possibly at The Hague (the center of international law in the Netherlands). The United Nations has a statement of human rights. I believe that we should look at that *very* closely.

VALUES

We can learn to be friends. The best way to make friends is to be a friend. I love my friends, and I am truthful, just, and committed to the best of my ability. Those values work together. Love means contributing to their growth, which first requires being truthful in the most positive way. I try to be fair and loyal in addition.

The universe unfolds based on truth. We never have the absolute truth, only our perception of it, which we call *knowledge.* Friends tell us the truth as they see it so that we can perceive choices and their likely consequences we might not otherwise see. Truth must be told in a way that is just, fair, and committed. The truth may hurt at first, but then it heals.

The healthiest thing for our own happiness is to seek truth and to reject old knowledge that is less true, making room for that which holds more truth. In this way, we obtain improved knowledge.

Justice? That's equality in how we are treated—no discrimination based on country of origin, race, religion, sex, age, etc.

These values all come in time. They are ideals. We need commitment. If we find values that make us happy, why give them up? Be committed to yourself first. (That means no suicide bombings, al-Qaeda. Don't you want to live to see your families grow and be happy and let others do the same? Is your religion making you so miserable that you feel it necessary to hurt others?)

Don't we want love, truth, justice, and commitment from our friends? The best way to gain something is to give it first. If it is not returned, at least you know that you tried your best. Mistakes are opportunities to learn. Insanity is defined as doing the same thing over and over again and expecting different results.

What about hate? We're human, so everyone can hate. I say that if we are to hate anything, that it is best that we hate *hate* itself. Release hate for living beings out of your system completely by talking or writing until you come to peace. And don't hate yourself. God doesn't hate anyone. Why should we hate ourselves?

There's a healthy hate where you stay far away from the hated object. Get out of the situation if you can. Then there's an unhealthy hate where you stay in the situation too long and you may possibly do things you are accountable for (if only in your conscience). My God is a loving God who forgives all sins—that is, if God exists. (I can't prove it either way.) But like John the Baptist said: repent! So that you may forgive yourself and earn others' forgiveness of you.

Some people say this is the end of days like it says in the Bible. Maybe it is. Maybe a Christ figure will arise to help the world save itself. And maybe there will be an Antichrist figure. I don't believe a Christ figure would slay the beast with a sword as it says in the Bible. He or she would believe as I do that the pen is mightier than the sword.

Many original religious books are old by definition. The universe is changing at every instant, and if we get anything out of religion, it should first be to grow love. Love yourself and your neighbor. Judaism, Christianity (which both advise us to love God and our neighbors), and Islam all refer to the same monotheistic God by one name or another—the God of Abraham: Allah, Jehovah, Yahweh, etc.

I don't blame God for what happens in nature, including earthquakes, tsunamis, volcanoes, plagues, and HIV (although human behavior may foster the latter). How we are born is biology. But the fact that we have life is a gift, and what we do with our lives are our gifts in return.

If we were created in God's image, then it seems to me that we were meant to try to become like God as much as humanly possible. We may hate what someone does, but we can love the sinner and hate the sin. We can try our best to separate the person from the act and forgive the person—at least within ourselves.

Talk or write about your hate in a nonviolent way. I don't believe in just turning the other cheek for more abuse. Rebuke the sinful person and—when they repent—forgive them. That repentance is more than saying, "Sorry. Please forgive me." It's a full confession, expressing remorse, making amends as much as possible, and explaining why they did it and why they see that it's in their own best interests not to do it again to you or anyone. If they do this, then you can trust that they've learned. We may forgive but not forget. Remember to get out of a harmful situation if you can. Fool me once, shame on you. Fool me twice, shame on me. If you're angry, get out of the situation until you can communicate in a calm, healthy manner. Commit first to yourself and then others. I commit to God first and foremost.

Does Jesus save? Yes, his words to love God and neighbor and self saved me. It's been said "God helps those that help themselves." Things that we can do nothing about we must learn to "give to God."

I don't believe that the United States is the *great Satan*. I believe there are evil acts and that there is no Satan. If God created the universe, why would God create Satan? Can people who believe that the United States performs evil acts write books about what they believe and distribute them here? Again, the pen is mightier than the sword.

So there's holy war, and there were the Crusades. Go ahead and have a war—a war of words. Write it down if no one will listen to you. Then possibly burn the paper. Crusade against more crusades. Terrorize the terrorists.

I have studied subatomic physics, nuclear physics, graduate-level optics, and much more. There's no end to it. Great, but please let's not destroy Mother Nature, other animals, insects, good germs and viruses, etc. A few people on earth could destroy it all. Wouldn't it be better to dedicate all our resources toward combating possible hostile aliens?

I plan to write a *Glenn Scott Allistair Simpson Coloring Book* that may in fact laugh at certain people at the highest levels of government.

Please realize that any religious book may have been subject to translation and interpretation and may have been altered to suit the interpreter's best interest (e.g., to control others, to brainwash others with dogma, and/or to elevate themselves to power). Go ahead and believe what you want, and let others do the same. You don't like the book *The Satanic Verses*? You don't have to read it. And no one should be forced to believe any religious book, including this one (even though I believe it is for everyone). I think doing otherwise is blasphemy.

Self-defense is justifiable. But aggressors, remember that a war can start with the act of just one person or one lie. No war is holy. War is war. We are holy. So is every life. And so is God, which is at the very least the totality of the universe.

Emotional costs of violence are passed down through generations. Heal yourself. Express your feelings verbally to others and through your representatives at the United Nations. Otherwise, you may have a psychological block. One American president said "the buck stops here." To the extent that you don't love someone else—you love yourself less. Miss no chance to love. This means unconditional love. The secret to happiness is not to find people to love you but rather to find opportunities to love everyone. Accept emotional and physical responsibility for your acts.

As I have written here, some say God is love. So loving God is loving love itself. How can that be wrong? Should one feel guilt after committing criminal acts of violence? Of course. We all have a conscience. Start by saying, "I am not a sinner. I am a human being who fully admits my guilt, and I will go to any length to pay for it." That's a human being.

So you can substitute the word *love* for God. We may love God and neighbor. We're all neighbors, not infidels. People change, but labels don't. Labels make a person easier to think about as a target, to dehumanize, and to control, but in truth, we are all human beings with the same basic rights and needs such as freedom and love, even though we think differently or occupy different space.

We don't have to think alike to love alike. We can all be on the side of love. Are we really ready to die for what we read in a book? Some are, including terrorists and suicide bombers. Our military teaches us to kill or be killed instead of loving thy neighbor as thyself. No wonder some veterans suffer from post-traumatic stress syndrome.

I heard that some suicide bombers may commit their final acts to receive money for their families. "The love of money is the root of all evil," as one said. People can love you back. Can money? No. Would your family rather have you dead than alive? What does that say about them?

Some believe they'll have seventy-two virgins in heaven if they kill themselves and take nonbelievers with them. Do you believe everything you hear or read? Will you jump off a roof because a book tells you to? (Hopefully not, but if you do, please don't hurt anyone else in the process.) In your religion, does your God really send to heaven people who commit suicide bombings? Extremist Muslim clerics, if you believe that these people will get seventy-two virgins in heaven, why don't you do it yourself instead of using pawns? ISIS, if others don't believe in your religion, do you want them to kill you (as you do others)? Remember the Golden Rule, which says, "Do unto others as you would have others do unto you." Then there is the Platinum Rule: "Do unto others as they would have done to themselves."

ISIS doesn't seem to want peace. It seems that they have invaded Syria and have fighters in the United States. I believe that we can make peace with them. It seems they want land, oil, or whatever. *Where there's life, there's hope.*

Happiness here and now can be a decision. If you're happy, do you really want to hurt anyone else? If you have seventy-two virgins, then you haven't chosen someone special to you to be in love with and marry (which is the best feeling in the world). Therefore, you can't help each grow toward God in a committed relationship (such as marriage). Don't we need to start with wanting our basic needs met instead of suicide and causing our families shame over their relatives having killed innocent people? These people aren't martyrs. The innocents are the martyrs. I believe the suicide bombers are misled and thereby become co-conspirators in their own self-destruction and that of others.

What about monogamy and marriage? What about being happily married to a real wife or husband and having a family on Earth and then possibly seeing each other in heaven? Isn't having seventy-two virgins adultery? And why do they have to be virgins? Do you believe that there are seventy-two times more women than men in heaven? Where did all those preponderant female souls come from? Why doesn't every woman receive seventy-two virgin men?

Some say, "No justice, no peace." Doesn't *no peace* also mean *no justice*? Consider going to the store to buy candy. Before the purchase, when you take that candy into your possession in the store, it's not just because the store proprietor owns it. Then you begin to pay for it with a bill larger than the price. That's unjust until you get your change. You get your change and your candy and now there is justice for everyone: it takes time and faith in the process.

Let's make a world of abundance together. If one of us fails, we may all lose. If you are not part of the solution, you are part of the problem.

Too much control is destructive—as is social competitiveness. Compete in business or sports, where everyone knows the rules. The free market makes sense, but treating people as capital doesn't. Money is good, but we can't eat it.

I read something a while ago about neurolinguistic programming. As I understand it, the words and sayings (ideas) we see and hear can have a bit of control over us. So think positively. Read positive things. Reject negatives actively. Try to listen to your feelings, and think outside the box. (One can think of books as boxes of sorts.) Think about the past that disturbs you, talk or write it out, and release the emotions nonviolently. The method of undoing suppressed emotions is to externalize unconscious conflicts and resolve them in peace. Inner peace comes with a clear conscience. If managed, conflict can lead to positive growth.

We've seen ISIS cutting people's heads off on the internet. From what I've heard, they are acting from what they've been told to do—something about defeating the enemy with the sword. Well, there's the maxim about loving thine enemy, and I interpret the *sword* as the *sharp word* or *tongue*. Discuss your issues with them and at the United Nations. If your religion is so great, shouldn't it be easy to convince people to convert without using force? Are you warriors—or robots without free will?

I've heard a story about two of the greatest martial artists being chosen for a contest to see whose skill was best. As the story goes, the two squared off for what seemed like an eternity. Finally, they bowed to each other and walked away because both of them knew that it would be the weaker one who would strike first. I've learned that when attacking, the attacker generally exposes a vulnerability.

Commit to your values. Elevate nonviolence first. Love is experienced from the inside and radiates out. Think about it. If you don't love yourself, can you be happy or help another be happy in the long term? It feels better to love than to hate. There is the term "cognitive dissonance" wherein things just don't feel right, even if our peers pressure us that what they want us to do is right. Give peace a chance.

Control/manipulation doesn't work in the long-term. It's wasted energy that leads to regret and guilt. We may offer people choices. That's a communication skill learned in anger management and assertiveness training.

Assertiveness makes use of the acronym DESC. *Describe* what you think went on between you. Then *express* how the other's behavior made you feel - in your body. The *S* stands for *specifying*, and the *C* stands for *choices* that the other can make. Each choice has consequences, and we can specify what we would prefer and how we'd expect to feel as a result of each decision the other may make. But if it hurts, get out of the situation if possible.

Remember that freedom entails responsibility. We are not responsible for the other person's actions—unless we coerce him or her. If we don't conquer fear, fear conquers us.

For those who have any doubts about the intentions of this book, please consider the following:

I am neither anti-American nor antireligion. I am against violence of any kind except in self-defense. I believe in equity— no discrimination based on race, sex, sexual orientation, religion, and the like. (Love is not an abomination.) I believe in equal opportunity and no harassment.

I respect differences in culture. I try to take an asking stance rather than assume anything based on my culture, wherein *culture* is everything learned. We can learn something from everyone. I just don't listen to verbal abuse and threats of physical harm. That hurts.

I attend Community Unitarian Universalist Church, which accepts the best ideas of all religions (Christianity, Judaism, Islam, Hindu, Buddhist, etc.) and nonreligious organizations (American Indian, atheism, agnostic, etc.). I embrace religious tolerance and the spirit of truth, and I am always on the side of love.

There were five US presidents who were Unitarian. Benjamin Franklin and other Founding Fathers were Unitarian. Abraham Lincoln had such leanings. And there was a US president who graduated from Duke.

I've also attended services at a Hindu temple, Protestant and Roman Catholic churches, and a synagogue. I intend to go to a mosque someday.

I believe in separation of church and state as well as checks and balances.

President Barack Obama ran on a platform of *change* and won. John F. Kennedy said, "Ask not what your country can do for you, but rather what you can do for your country." And I say to you and your neighbor and the rest of the world, "Help others. It helps you." It's always a relationship, and when the other grows, you may have the best chance to grow - with the other if you stay in the relationship.

Are we happy when we see videos of children starving to death and suffering from diseases? We can try to help them, but if parents won't practice birth control and monogamy, thus leading to more children without two-parent households, they might be taxed (as I've heard occurs in China). If people who want to have children in areas of overpopulation had only one child, the problem would be better addressed.

One Russian philosopher said, "The power of ideas is greater than the use of force," and he was right. If people are pointing weapons at you and if you can help change their ideas, they may not use those arms, and you may help them, too. Perhaps they are pointing at you in the hope that you will help them. "How can I help?" you may ask. You can help them live on without a guilty conscience. Let your conscience be your guide. They may turn out to be some of your best friends. Seek to help those who would harm you, or they may become prisoners of their own minds. The truth shall set you free. Physical maladies may be caused in part by emotional and psychological stress because of guilt.

It's been said that power corrupts, and absolute power corrupts absolutely. But there is no absolute power except that of God—if there is one or even if there are many.

Will there be checks and balances in a united world government just like in the United States? Of course. The world leader would ultimately report to God … and everyone else.

MENTAL HEALTH

I have worked on Wall Street and in other for-profit industries, government agencies, and not-for-profits. I currently work in the mental health field.

When dealing with others, the mental health field promotes being person-centered by asking people about their hopes and dreams and working together to attain them. Put their interests first. Isn't the therapy for them? Mental health care should also be strength-based by focusing on abilities rather than weaknesses. These ideals work in all interpersonal relationships.

Mental health practitioners should be recovery-oriented, and they should believe that people can recover from their personal problems, which is often recovery from trauma. We can all begin recovery from trauma now if needed. After all, we don't want traumas to get worse – which may happen if left untreated. Learn the traumas of others. Let them speak. Ask them if you think it is appropriate. Everyone has their own unique story, and we must respect that.

We're not responsible for the acts of others. They act on their own free will. In that case, we needn't blame ourselves. The shame belongs to the other, not ourselves. Some victims blame themselves for being mistreated – even to the extent of identifying with the victimizers – blocking the recovery.

Some people with psychological problems project them onto others and punish them for those issues (psychopathology). Sadism and masochism go together. I believe that a person with sadistic tendencies can also be masochistic toward themselves. Sexual sadomasochism is okay if it's a mutual choice. But when it causes harm, that's where I disagree.

Talk about behavior, not about labeling people. Use the humanistic approach without the psychiatric labels. Most importantly, are people violent or making threats of violence to themselves or others? Then they rate on a negative scale, say from minus ten to zero of a new scale (someone like Hitler would be minus ten). Those who are functional and nonviolent can go up to ten. Complete recovery is possible. Instead of the *Diagnostic and Statistical Manual of Mental Disorders (DSM-5)* in psychiatry. People who hear those labels therein (such as "schizophrenic") applied to them may take it to their grave. Psychiatrists can only observe behavior – they can't read minds.

It is said that schizophrenia often involves psychosis, which often is displayed as paranoia, which always has an element of truth to it. And it is said that paranoia involves delusions of grandeur and persecution. They cannot be separated. I prefer to simply say that I either agree or disagree with certain people's words rather than labeling them because labels can aggravate the clients' problems and worsen the stigma. I've read that in third world countries, people with schizophrenia often get better over time with no medication. I've read that some medications can cause thoughts of hostility and suicide. And the patients aren't warned. Who really cares about them anyway? I do. The person must be monitored by a professional, and the benefits must outweigh the risks for the patient, not the psychiatrist.

Any organism under enough stress will break down. So please don't blame or shame people for problems they did not cause. In the past, society at large and family interactions were seen as the causes of mental illness. Psychiatry is a relatively young science. The first psychiatrists drilled holes in people's heads to let out the "evil spirits." And don't forget that in Salem, *witches* were burned at the stake for having "the evil eye." The word *crazy* means that we ourselves do not understand.

Words (and labels) can do more harm than acts. Words can damage one on a psychological and emotional level, and cause further trauma. One can see physical scars and bruises. It's harder to see the harm of words.

I've read that "the mentally ill are the misunderstood." I believe a person's condition is generally a mental injury (not illness) that's often perpetuated by the system. They are more often the victims of—rather than perpetrators of—violent crime. They are less violent than the general population. I've learned that alcohol is often associated with violent crime and that guns in the home are more often used during an argument against people the gun owner actually knows (family members and friends), especially when alcohol is involved.

It has been said, "Any society that does not put the rights of the individual first is doomed for failure." And another saying states, "The measure of any society is how it treats the least fortunate of its individuals."

I have seen no less fortunate in the United States than the homeless, so-called mentally ill injured war veteran. I believe that we could offer these people a respite—a place of supportive shelter, a home away from home to get back on their feet, a place to come and go instead of forced psychiatric hospitalization and medication, which can be traumatic, disruptive, and much more expensive. All of that can make people afraid to get help when they actually need it. As with any medication, there are side effects. Of course, if there's imminent danger of physical harm to the self or others, involuntary confinement and medication may be necessary. During these days many in this country view themselves as victims of the thought police and the police state. Although there are excellent ones, psychiatrists and mental hospitals are not always person-centered. Big Pharma has a vested interest in medicine. Let's not forget about healing talk therapy.

Depression is anger turned inward. There's no shame or blame in that. Recovery is always possible.

Let's take the term *mental illness.* How about being positive and understand the degrees of mental wellness? Even some the writers of *DSM-5* are rejecting their own books. It's getting so big. It's like having a category for every person. Every person has their own unique story and is not just a category or a statistic. It's a fallacy in logic to appeal to authority and assume they are right no matter what. The experts disagree.

I believe that it's a fact that many if not all can recover from emotional and psychological problems, and they can stop using illegal and addictive prescription drugs and alcohol (and hopefully psychotropics) over time with the help of a psychiatrist. I've heard that research has shown that after seven years on antipsychotics, people often do better in their recovery without the medication. Again, if the time comes, one may want to taper off—with the help of a psychiatrist—in six months or so for each medication (according to a federal agency I consulted with). To tell people that they must take a medication for the rest of their lives also mandates that they see psychiatrists for the rest of their lives too. I think the best practitioners are those who see their job as working themselves out of a job.

I've heard that the so-called "chemical imbalance in the brain" is not found before treatment but rather after the treatment with medication has begun. Then there is an imbalance because the medication causes the brain to overproduce to compensate for the neurochemicals that are blocked by the medication. If the medication is stopped abruptly, it causes the person to experience symptoms that are worse than those when they started the medication because of the overproduction.

After recovery from the trauma, there's a mental disability because that person is reliant on the medication even though there is no *illness*. I am not a psychiatrist, so please consult one to be sure, but I believe there's hope that a person may slowly be weaned off the medication with the help of a psychiatrist. There's hope for a full recovery. That's why we must discard the stigma of suffering with mental health issues. Then those who need help are more likely to ask for it. Of course, patients may want to be hospitalized and take medication for the rest of their lives. I just hope that they are given a choice and informed of the consequences of each. There is something known as the "practitioner's illusion": the practitioner falsely believes those with mental illness never recovery – because they only see those patients who come back (not those who recover and never come back).

Would you get along with yourself if you were another person, such as your spouse, parents, children, friends, coworkers, or neighbors? If so, there's no need to change.

The terms *nuts*, and *psycho* just refer to the fact that we don't understand.

Of course, there is psychopathic behavior, but if the person isn't violent, it may be understandable why they may have violent *thoughts*. It may just be a normal reaction to an abnormal circumstance. We can offer help, but sometimes they just need time alone to think things out and reflect. God heals all wounds.

THE SOLUTION

The United Nations is an indication that most of the world wants to cooperate to work toward their stated goal— happiness. The sin lies not in failing to reach this goal but in not setting the goal high enough. I don't know, but I think God doesn't want anyone to die prematurely as in the case of suicide or homicide. I believe God wants us to see his will be done and for each of us to live as peacefully, lovingly, happily, and joyfully as long and as much as possible. And wants us to go forth and prosper. If not, who needs that book (the Bible or whatever)?

We may attempt to do God's will for our own good, not because of anything we read in a book, even this one. God is inside of us and created us. Listen to your feelings. Think. Feel. Act. Listen to your conscience, and let it guide your way. Do more than survive. Thrive. A famous American patriot named Patrick Henry said, "Give me liberty or give me death." Free yourself from the past.

If you believe that humankind created God and not vice versa, fine. You may still want to be at peace, loving, happy, and joyous.

I hope that I haven't scared anyone off. We must take baby steps at first to build a world government, starting in the United States. Babies learn more in a shorter amount of time than adults because they don't self-criticize but simply observe. Let's not assume the worst. Relaxed concentration is required to complete complex tasks. Trust but verify. Let's not engage in self-judgment (as we may learn in Zen Buddhism).

Never say never. Edmund Burke wrote, "The only thing necessary for the triumph of evil is for good men to do nothing." The best revenge is to live your life well.

I believe God's love, truth, justice, and commitment to us all wins in the end. You certainly don't have to, but it works for me.

When we are attacked, we can choose to fight, flight, or freeze. We learn the most when we freeze. It appears to be a slump from an outsider's perspective, but it's unlearning old behavior and replacing it with new behavior. Ultimately leading to most positive growth.

Eventually, the world leader may represent Earth to other possible life-forms. If male, we might call that person the master of the universe (all universes big and small).

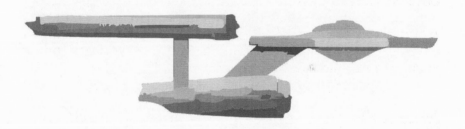

I imagine that the world leader may lead (not dominate) the leaders of each country, but at some point we must all lead ourselves as best we are able. I believe that by doing so, we can all help make a heaven on Earth and enable more leaders. Let's get our priorities right. Let's try to act as a team with a goal of world peace.

When stressed, one's internal activation level is raised. This increased energy can be used positively (as in hitting a tennis ball) or destructively in anger (as in breaking the racquet). The degree of stress of a stressor is based on the perception of that stress. If you perceive that a tiger on television is not a threat, there's little stress. Simple tasks such as passing buckets in a bucket brigade for putting out a fire require increased adrenaline. Complex tasks typically require a relaxed form of concentration.

The English first settled America to escape religious persecution. What they did to the American Indians and slaves was shameful. Let's make sure the American Indian has an opportunity to succeed now. Let's invest in our children and future generations by investing in schools in downtrodden areas. Perhaps we can also teach some of the principles outlined in this book in philosophy or ethics classes at the schools. Teach students nonviolent communication and the objective meaning of words such as *love, peace, happiness,* and *joy*. It's not religion. *God* is a word in the dictionary and has a definition as well. Some people believe that humankind created God. Let them believe whatever they want to but not act in violence.

When negotiating, try to bring up all the issues that all parties have from the beginning, and try to agree on as much as possible. Or you can agree to disagree. And then you move on to another issue. If we address bigger issues first, the smaller issues will likely take care of themselves.

"Love, faith, and hope abide, and the greatest of these is love." Wherever possible, choose the path that's more loving. There is always a way. *Love thine enemy.*

As I have written herein, some religions predict that a world leader of a world government will rise and be the Antichrist (a make-believe beast). Why? Are the authors clairvoyant? Before that happens (if it does at all), I believe there will be a reincarnation of Christ, the coming of Maitreya Buddha, an avatar of Krishna, or the Messiah in Judaism. Believe whatever you wish as long as you don't hurt anyone physically, emotionally, or psychologically in the process.

ISIS, please stop beheading people, burning others alive, and crucifying children. The children are not responsible for the actions of prior generations. Unless you want war, give the accused fair trials and don't torture. Al-Qaeda, please stop the suicide bombings and terrorism. You may live to regret them. God sees everything. The Jewish people didn't kill Christ. The Romans did. The Romans falsely decided on Jesus's guilt and falsely proclaimed him to be the "king of the Jews." I never saw it written that he said that. They all had a choice not to crucify him, even if the Jewish people decided on Jesus's sentence. Everyone was wrong except Jesus. There were dictators who gave orders and did not listen. Crucifixion was for the worst of criminals. Here in the United States, we have due process of the law, and we do not support cruel or unusual punishment. We have the right to appeal and stand before a jury of our peers. It wasn't the devil in the crowd of the Jewish people. All the people were acting of their own free will, which was given by God. Let's learn from their mistakes and not repeat them in any way. If we did, Jesus would have died in vain. Dr. Martin Luther King Jr. said, "Injustice anywhere is injustice everywhere." Some people say that we are in hell right now. I imagine all of us bringing heaven to Earth.

The universe is changing every instant. Consider all the atoms and elementary particles in the ever-expanding universe. Do we change with it, or are we too stubborn? Life is for the living.

People sometimes oversimplify and say that "everything is relative" (according to Albert Einstein). Relative is relative. Everything doesn't matter as much as your relatives and we all came from the same ones. I heard on television that the DNA remains of the first woman on earth were discovered, further proving my point. We are all family.

As I wrote before, happiness is not being loved by others but rather finding the way to love all people. Yes, that includes Adolf Hitler and Osama bin Laden. It would have been better had those men obeyed their consciences and not killed. Crimes must be punished. No one is above the law. But separate the person from the act. Seek to understand before seeking to be understood. I believe in defending yourself, upholding the law, and protecting the innocent.

Physics is the most fundamental study of nature (as I studied at Clarkson University in Potsdam, New York). That includes advanced calculus (differential equations), cosmology, quantum mechanics, special and general relativity, graduate optics, elementary particles, black hole research, astronomy, astrophysics, space science, thermal physics, grand unified field theory, and group theory (and later string theory and the so-called search for the "God particle"). My studies in psychology included an introduction to psychology, learning and motivation, stress management, and abnormal psychology. Also came philosophy, the philosophy of science, logic and analytical reasoning (rhetoric).

At Duke, I studied financial and managerial accounting, finance, marketing, introductory and advanced statistics, manufacturing strategy, organizational behavior, public policy, operations, negotiations, investments, short-run finance, and management game simulation. (We reported to a real board.) I was chosen by the former presidential advisor from the navy to teach business computer laboratory sections in the first executive MBA program, which became ranked number one in the world a few years.

Physics is the most fundamental study of nature. Psychology is the most fundamental study of humankind. Business is how humans interact with one another and nature to maximize profit. But we shouldn't profit at all costs. It must be legal. There needs to be love, peace, happiness, and joy.

My economics professor at Duke—another former presidential advisor—taught our class that researchers have come up with the idea that organizations are really trying to maximize utility (above profit), which translates into "happiness," he said.

Above business is politics. Then comes religion. Our love is more important than our faith or what book we go by. Beyond religion is philosophy. We choose how to live our lives.

Rather than seventy-two virgins in heaven, wouldn't a member of al-Qaeda be happier to fall in love, marry a real virgin (or not) on earth, make love, and have children rather than turning himself into a weapon of mass destruction? Do members of al-Qaeda think they are going to have orgasms in heaven without bodies? The best we can expect is to be with the Holy Spirit when we pass as members of one family in the kingdom of heaven. There may not be a hell, but there may be a purgatory where we must pay for our crimes. "The wages of sin is death." Indeed, we may only live once. Personally, I believe that we live forever and that every action—or inaction—has consequences.

Marriage is all about communication. It's a promise to love each other forever. Let's find a country to propose to. If you're desperate to marry, marry God. (Priests do, and I have too.) Then you can marry someone else who also married God if you would like.

I don't like the term *Jew*. To me, it's *Jewish*. Whether Christian, Muslim, Buddhist, or Hindu, we are people first and not sinners or infidels. I don't believe that we are all sinners (original sin) and that everything that we do is a sin. How depressing. That just brings needless guilt. We can only do our best, and we had no choice about being born in the first place, let alone what race we were born as.

I think that religion should be a choice and that there shouldn't be any discrimination. Labeling makes things easier to think about. But every person is different in their practice—or their lack of practice—of religion.

In the Bible, it is written, "I Am." Then a most powerful mathematical identity I came upon long ago while writing in a journal. (I believe it was given to me by God in my despair.) Consider: "I am I." You are you. You are yourself, and I am myself. And I am a friend to everyone to the best of my ability. Other people who are not my friends are potential friends. You are not so much male or female as you are an individual. We must have equality of the sexes.

The choice of peace and violence are set before us. I recommend peace and love over hate. (Hate doesn't feel good, does it?). Choose to be happy rather than unhappy, and be joyous.

Is this anarchy? No, this is just a recommendation for positive change with all the due respect for our current systems (e.g., freedom of speech and press, freedom to choose, and the freedom to vote in your best interests).

When you love people who are guilty of crimes, you simply want what is best for them. You want them to stop participating in criminal activity, to repent, and to earn our forgiveness (and perhaps their own). Punishment is tough love by taking away a positive, not by inflicting something negative. The latter type of punishment doesn't work. Violence in people must also be stopped for their own protection and for their own conscience.

Play nicely with others. Some children act badly for attention. In some cases, it's the only way they can get attention. Please do not try to take justice into your own hands (except when you must defend yourself). "Eye for an eye" justice leaves everyone blind. Violence begets violence.

If people say something against the Quran, listen. You might learn something. There are other books too. It's not their fault that those people who kill them can't listen to what may reveal more truth. It's a book, and saying something against it isn't personal. Criticism is not an assault and is not blasphemy. It's a discussion. It's called learning and growing toward God. Muhammad may have been great, but that doesn't mean someone won't come along and say and do greater. I believe extremist followers of Islam believe that Christ will come back and lead armies to achieve their goals. What about Christ's goal to love God and your neighbor? With that goal, we'd need no armies—except to deliver food, shelter, clothing, medicine, and security at the very least.

Try loving everyone, including past, present, and future generations, especially yourself. Give it a try and see how it goes!

CONCLUSION

If you decide that you agree with enough of this and want to be more peaceful, loving, happy, and joyous than you are right now, I hope you'll consider me for president of the United States of America and eventually world leader (if that position ever exists). I've heard it said that a president is often judged by his or her character.

In the meantime, three years ago I mailed a manuscript of this book to the White House in the hope of becoming a presidential advisor. I also mailed a copy to the Secretary General of the United Nations in the hope of becoming a consultant. I've also mailed it to the Duke University Press in the hope of publication. Unfortunately, I've had no luck yet.

Help me help you. I don't need your vote. You need your vote. That's why it was given to you. Or if you're not of age yet, it hopefully will be given to you soon.

I just hope the next president does what he or she can do to help you feel at peace; loving; happy; and joyous in this world, our country, state, county, city, town, village, church, or whatever. Campaign against violence. No child should suffer abuse or neglect. No person should suffer rape or incest either.

I practice Unitarian Universalism, which was founded partly on the principle that everyone goes to heaven and there is no hell. I am spiritual. I am also a member of Mensa (top 2 percent of people with high IQs in the world). I am the exactly the same as you, the reader, in God's eyes.

I would try to have answers in terms of ISIS, Syria, Russia having built nuclear weapons in the Arctic Circle, North Korea and President Trump exchanging "love letters" (as he said) with Kim Jung-un (and his supplying nuclear fuel to Iran), relations of US to Iran, racial relations in the US, and more. I just need the position, if you will.

My father, a nonpracticing Episcopalian (of Irish, Scottish, and Scandinavian heritage), told me when I was young that "Jews came from black." I say that we are all black in the pupils of our eyes. My mother was nonpracticing Jewish, but she hid that fact for fear of discrimination in our region back in her day. I have been confronted with fairly heavy discrimination, hate, and violence, but thank God I am okay now.

My father told me to "never marry a Jew." He was anti-Semitic, perhaps even toward his own children. In Christianity, if the father is Christian, so are the children. My parents were both racist toward blacks. (I say *black* because they discriminated against all people with that color skin, not just African Americans.) I am not racist at all. I am against all racism. I've been told that my mother's parents were from Russia and Lithuania. But I learned from DNA testing that I am just more than 1 percent Nigerian, East Asian, and North African each, despite my light skin and blue eyes. Maybe you will become a world leader someday. Who knows?

I guess I'd have to say that my heritage is a hybrid. I am an agent of change.

The whole world loses when even one person is hurt. Ever hear of the "butterfly effect"? If you believe in Adam and Eve, are we not all family? If you don't believe that, perhaps you think we all come from the same amoeba.

"There is no greater love than this: that one lays down their life for a friend."

You are loved.

I wish you peace, love, happiness, and joy!

NOTES

I recommend that you vote as your heart desires! If I am not selected as a candidate, I believe that you can write in my name on the ballot.

My name is Glenn Simpson, but there are many people (perhaps many women) with that name too. My full legal name is Glenn Scott Allistair Simpson. Perhaps you may want to write or call your elected representatives in the federal and state government if you agree with any of my ideas. Perhaps you may want to even send a postcard to save on stamps, especially if you can't afford a telephone.

I also wish you the very best (even if I don't make it in 2020 race or thereafter). Some say that Jesus saves. His words that we should love God and our neighbor saved me. Through my media specialist consultant and the marketing of my printed books and e-book, I will try to find you to say hello.

And by the way, dear reader, you need not buy my very next title, *Peace, Love, Happiness, and Joy for God's Universe.* It contains many of the same ideas inside it as this one. I guess you could say this one is a Trojan horse for nonbelievers, agnostics, Buddhists, and others. Or you can buy a copy to start a collection. I intend to keep writing as long as I live because I love it so much! I've been asked by both of these two publishers to write series, so I'll see what I can do. I hope you can afford my coloring book, which should come out soon! It will be available through Barnes & Noble, Amazon, and perhaps other places.

Peace, love, happiness, and joy to you and yours!